DES INDEP ͏ENCE, INSPIRATION, *and* INNOVATION

70 YEARS

The New York State Association of Independent Schools at 70

DESIGN FOR INDEPENDENCE, INSPIRATION, *and* INNOVATION

70 YEARS

The New York State Association of Independent Schools at 70

DANE L. PETERS

Published by The New York State Association
of Independent Schools
Albany, NY

Design for Independence, Inspiration, and Innovation: The New York State Association of Independent Schools at 70, by Dane L. Peters

Published by The New York State Association of Independent Schools, 17 Elk Street (First Floor), Albany, NY 12207, (518) 694-5500. E-mail: info@nysais.org. Website: *www.nysais.org.*

Printed in the United States of America.

ISBN: 978-0-692-90643-9
Design, Typography, and Setup: Custom Communications, Inc., Saco, ME

Photo Credits: Front cover: Depositphotos Inc.; back cover: iStock by Getty Images; Chapter 4, p. 57: Livestream logo; Chapter 5, p. 60: Karjalainen, Claire, "Mentoring: Cross-Generational Mentorship: Why Age Should Be No Object," *Modern Workforce by Everwise.* All other photos courtesy of The New York State Association of Independent Schools.

10 9 8 7 6 5 4 3 2 1

To the many volunteers who have provided ongoing support and to the innovative, dedicated NYSAIS staff.

CONTENTS

FOREWORD

Since Collegiate School was founded in New York in 1628, independent schools have been growing in number and thriving in the United States. While there are many attributes that make independent schools unique—great teachers, focus on the whole child, high academic standards, and inclusiveness—it is that very independence that sets them apart in the education landscape. Independent schools have the power to create educational experiences that meet each child's needs, without state mandates on curriculum, textbooks, and testing.

Another element that makes independent schools strong is the power of a *community* of independence—a community of schools with unique missions that unite around a common vision of support and growth for the individual child. This is what makes independent education a uniquely powerful force in American education today. The glue for these communities is the associations—local, state, regional, national, and international—that support the needs of schools and the people who run them. These range from loosely established social networks of educators to larger trade associations that serve all constituents within independent schools.

According to the American Society for Association Executives (ASAE), there are close to 67,000 associations in the United States and one in three Americans belongs to an association. They do so because associations play a powerful role in American society. They improve structures and systems, enhance skills and create opportunities, and strengthen lives. This year, we celebrate the New York State Association of Independent Schools

(NYSAIS) for its 70 years of service to independent schools. Over that time, it has led and supported independent schools through its accreditation, professional learning and development services, informational resources, and advisory services.

Never has the kind of support that NYSAIS provides been more important to schools. The education landscape is transforming, and keeping up with and interpreting those shifts is more than a full-time job for any school administrator. The demographic make-up of the student population is changing dramatically; the economic buying power and consumer attitudes about what constitutes a quality education are shifting; and the kinds of education options available to students are growing exponentially. Even more perplexing is the notion that we are now educating students for a world that will undoubtedly be different from the world today in ways we can't even imagine. Associations like NYSAIS and the one that I represent, the National Association of Independent Schools (NAIS), work hard together to track, interpret, and strategize around these trends so that independent schools can continue to thrive amid such change.

Also crucial today is the act of focusing a lens on school operations so that school leaders can understand where and when they need to flex in order to be the best they can be. Services such as accreditation, which NYSAIS has been offering since 1969, can be a lever for affirming mission and vision, identifying strengths and opportunities for improvement, and launching innovations. Further, a rigorous accreditation process can signal to parents that a school offers a high-quality education and is constantly challenging itself to become better.

The quickly changing cultural and educational landscape, of course, also means that we need talented leaders. Leading a school today is more challenging than it was even a decade ago. It can also be an isolating experience. Thus, getting support to learn and grow throughout the journey is crucial for a leader's survival. Associations like NYSAIS offer a lifeline to leaders through networking opportunities in small peer groups or through larger gatherings such as conferences, workshops, and institutes. Also, school advisory services, such as NYSAIS's Experienced Leaders Advising Schools (ELAS) program, can provide just-in-time help as schools confront challenges or embrace opportunities. Access to knowledge and expertise when you need it is essential at a time when the rate of change keeps accelerating.

Communities also have the power to drive societal change. If you think of a school at a center of a circle that keeps expanding outward through its affiliations, you begin to see the power of independence multiplied. Through our collective actions, we have preserved independence so that each child can thrive in the way best suited to his or her individual learning style, driven legislation that supports an equitable and just society, and protected the charitable deduction so that money can flow to independent schools in support of high-quality programs.

I recently read an article by a Seattle-based coach, Jen Waak, about the power of community in helping us achieve tough goals. She made the point that community is important because it:

- Gives us access to collective wisdom.
- Helps us to push our limits.
- Supports us and believes in us.
- Brings us new ideas.
- Holds us accountable.

As NYSAIS celebrates its anniversary, I want to commend the organization for bringing the power of community to the

196 schools and 84,000 students it serves. NYSAIS lives at the crossroads of independence and community serving our schools as they need it today and as they prepare for the future.

Happy 70th!

Donna Orem
President, NAIS

PREFACE

At its core, NYSAIS has always been about relationships. This was true in 1947 when Paul D. Shafer from the Packer Collegiate Institute sent out a letter to ten colleagues suggesting that they meet to discuss the formation of a statewide independent school organization. This was also true when that first annual meeting was held at the Emma Willard School in Troy as well as subsequent annual meetings in the Capital Region—all emphasizing the statewide nature of this fledgling organization. In fact, the first NYSAIS executive director, Appleton Mason, located the first NYSAIS offices in Loudonville, outside of Albany, to ensure that schools across the entire state felt included.

This commitment to relationships continued when NYSAIS began holding its annual meetings at Mohonk Mountain House in 1978 under the leadership of Executive Director Steve Hinrichs. And today, seventy years since NYSAIS's founding, this commitment to relationships continues through the efforts of Barbara Swanson, Diana Wahrlich, Maria Flores Seibert, Judy Sheridan, George Swain, and Andrew Cooke. Recognizing the important role that relationships play within the NYSAIS community, the NYSAIS staff spends a considerable amount of its professional time working with the hundreds of volunteers who help NYSAIS fulfill its place as an independent school advocate throughout the State of New York as well as throughout the country.

We see it as our job, of course, to help each and every member school. But we also see it as our job to contribute to the national conversation on independent education. As Donna

Orem, president of NAIS, acknowledges in her Foreword, "The independent school world is undergoing profound changes that will shape our world for decades to come."

While technology will continue to play a pivotal and expanding role in NYSAIS's ability to communicate and fully engage with members throughout the state, the foundational commitment to relationships should never be forgotten. Those of us who are fortunate enough to be involved in the life of NYSAIS in 2017 will continue to build on the strong work of our predecessors, cognizant of our profound responsibility to those who will come after us. This book, therefore, serves as a snapshot of NYSAIS in 2017 and a call to action as NYSAIS looks forward to the next seventy years.

Our deepest thanks go to Dane Peters for documenting the history of NYSAIS in his first book *Independent by Design* and for creating this second book for our 70th anniversary. A special thanks goes to retired NYSAIS head of school, and former NYSAIS board chair, Steve Clement, for volunteering to serve as the chair of this 70th-anniversary celebration. We are deeply indebted to those who came before and those who will come after. Happy 70th anniversary to the NYSAIS community of independent school educators!

Mark W. Lauria, Ph.D.
Executive Director, NYSAIS

INTRODUCTION

In 2014, I published *Independent by Design,* a history of the New York State Association of Independent School (NYSAIS) from its inception in 1947 to 2014. I can imagine a reader asking why I'd work on a new volume about NYSAIS just three years later. The answer is twofold. For one, the past three years represent a period of significant organizational growth and development. This new level of momentum and focus has not only established NYSAIS as a thought-leader in the field, operating at a high level among independent school associations worldwide, it also comes at a time when education itself is undergoing a significant tectonic shift. That this surge also comes at a time when NYSAIS is celebrating its seventieth anniversary makes it all that more noteworthy.

One way to look at this volume is as an important postscript to the earlier volume. But it also serves as the opening chapter of NYSAIS's next seventy years of operation. The ability of the organization to make significant adjustments in an era of deep social change and disruption while staying true to its seventy-year-old mission is a clear sign of a healthy organizational future.

To say our current era is interesting would be an understatement. There are a number of forces at work, of course. But a key one is the way multiple generations, with their particular mindsets, overlap and interact. When I was first teaching, for instance, we lived in a world essentially of three generations—The Greatest Generation, Baby Boomers, and Generation X. Today, our world is five generations strong—The Greatest Generation, Baby Boomers, Generation X, Millennials (Generation

Y), and Generation Z. For a long time, the Baby Boomers more or less called the shots, but the shift is now on—with the Baby Boomers moving into retirement and the younger generations having both a greater presence and greater influence. And all signs suggest that this influence will only get stronger. Writing for the *Independent School* magazine blog in 2016, NAIS president-elect Donna Orem underscored this ongoing shift in leadership. "'Who will lead' is a refrain we hear routinely in the media as the workforce changes hands from the Baby Boomers and Generation X to the Millennials," she writes. "The leading edge of the Baby Boomer generation reached retirement age in 2011. According to the Pew Research Center, 10,000 Boomers will retire each day through the year 2030." [1]

This generational shift also corresponds with the dizzying rise of technological innovation. Technology is changing just about everything in our culture, including communications, manufacturing, the workplace environment, entertainment, shopping, and, of course, education.

The schools that NYSAIS serves are all multigenerational. They all wrestle with the shifts in education brought on in part by technology, by brain-science research, and by changing cultural perspectives about the role of education in society. For its part, NYSAIS is influenced by all of this—and the progress it makes every day is testimony to the attentiveness and hard work of the staff.

Design for Independence, Inspiration, and Innovation: The New York State Association of Independent Schools at 70 presents the changes that have taken place over the past three years within the organization. Granted, this is a short time period, but NYSAIS's seventieth anniversary and the rapid, impressive changes are more than enough justification for this book—as a birthday celebration, as testimony to the hard work of the current staff, and as an exploration of the evolving role of school associations.

A quick review of the history of this association reveals a history of valuable service—of moving both schools and the field of education forward. From its inception in 1947 to the present, NYSAIS has been dedicated to building strong schools through professional development for its member schools, faculty, and staff. Today, NYSAIS's central strength is in its staff—a staff that continues to model love of organization through hard work and relentless dedication to the mission of the organization.

NYSAIS Facts at a Glance

Here are the basics facts about NYSAIS today:

- It is the second largest state/regional independent school association in the country.
- It serves just under 200 member schools and organizations. Among those:
    - 116 schools in New York City
    - 20 on Long Island
    - 13 in Capital District
    - 13 in Lower Hudson Valley
    - 13 in Westchester County
    - 12 in Western Lakes
    - 2 in Lake Placid
    - 1 in Syracuse
    - 1 in Cooperstown
    - 1 in Istanbul, Turkey
- The schools vary widely in focus:
    - 62 with religious affiliation
    - 24 with boarding programs
    - 19 with programs for special needs students

- 16 that are all boys
- 14 that are all girls
- NYSAIS member schools educate more than 84,000 students. [2]

The core work of serving its members has remained constant, of course, but it is interesting to examine the way the organization's mission has evolved over its long history.

At its 20th annual meeting in November 1968 and "[w]ith its provisional charter, brand-new executive secretary, and an office," NYSAIS was, after twenty short years, ready to embrace its autonomy; but a couple of things had to fall into place before that could happen. First of all, its provisional charter required that a constitution and board of trustees be put into place, and that is exactly what was voted on during this annual meeting. Of special importance was the NYSAIS Constitution's Article II, which outlined the association's mission:

> *The purpose of the organization shall be to promote the independence and well-being of and public regard for the independent schools of the State of New York; to safeguard the interests of these schools in the matter of legislation and regulation; to foster mutually beneficial relations with the New York State Education Department and other educational agencies; to serve as the New York State member association of the National Association of Independent Schools; to assist member schools in maintaining standards of excellence; to encourage activities for the purpose of keeping our education work updated and current; to provide service and leadership to the communities of which we are a part.* [3]

Fast-forward forty-three years, and the NYSAIS mission is not only simplified, it has added its significant new role as an accrediting body. At the same time, the mission is clarified through the addition of organizational principles—including greater interaction with the public school sector.

MISSION STATEMENT

(Approved by the NYSAIS Board of Trustees on November 2, 2011)

The New York State Association of Independent Schools promotes the independence, well-being and public understanding of, and respect for, New York independent schools and serves as an accrediting body chartered by the New York State Board of Regents.

Throughout the book, you will notice overlapping concepts. On the one hand, I write about the impact of technology on the organization's core services to schools. On the other hand, I look at that technology's impact on schools themselves. For instance, I write about the association's dynamic video and livestream service, NYSAIS-*Now*. It was conceived and grew up under the organization's technology leadership, but its greatest impact is on teacher and administrator professional development. You will notice a similar overlapping experience when you read about generational differences.

NYSAIS ORGANIZATIONAL PRINCIPLES

In order to accomplish its mission, the New York State Association of Independent Schools:

- Establishes the criteria, which reflect the values and best educational practices for evaluating and accrediting member schools.
- Promotes professional growth of teachers, administrators, and trustees through workshops, conferences, and exchanges.
- Informs and counsels the leadership at member schools in matters of legislation and regulation.
- Facilitates the development of cooperative projects among member schools and between member schools and public schools.
- Fosters mutually beneficial relations with the New York State Education Department, the National Association of Independent Schools, other educational associations, and the general public.
- Informs member schools about significant practices and developments in independent education.
- Provides such other services as will benefit the member schools and the communities they serve. [4]

It is also important to note that NYSAIS is made up of individual departments that take care of a dynamic membership, but that also operate collectively as a well-organized system, integrating technology, accreditation, business management, professional development, and other essential member services. The same holds true for NYSAIS among other state and regional associations, including the National Association of Independent Schools (NAIS) in its dedication to cooperate, support, and promote exemplary educational practices throughout the country.

When you think about the responsibility of an education association like NYSAIS—supporting 196 schools and organizations and 84,000 students *every year*, and operating in a time of near dizzying social, economic, and technological change—it's hard not to look at the work of the bright, knowledgeable, dedicated NYSAIS staff with anything but awe.

A NYSAIS staff-meeting arrangement as it looks today.

DESIGN FOR INDEPENDENCE, INSPIRATION, AND INNOVATION

CHAPTER ONE

Finding the Virtual and Personal Balance

In the early 1950s, NYSAIS was a one-person operation—the executive director working out of his home. By the 1980s, it grew to a three-person office at the Emma Willard School in Troy. Today, NYSAIS has a staff of seven, but only two are based full-time at the office in Albany (17 Elk Street, first floor). The other five work primarily out of their homes spread across the state. This telecommuting arrangement is a result of what the NYSAIS budget allows and what technology enables. But it is also what has kept the staff stable over the years and has enabled much of the innovative programming at NYSAIS.

In his book *Drive: The Surprising Truth About What Motivates Us*, Daniel Pink tells us that autonomy in the workplace is one of three principles that motivate people. To demonstrate his point, he relays the story of Cali Ressler and Jody Thompson, two former human resources executives at the American retailer Best Buy who developed what they call "a results-only work environment"—or ROWE for short. "In a ROWE work-place, people don't have schedules," Pink writes. "They show up when they want. They don't have to be in the office at a certain time—or any time, for that matter. They just have to get their work done. How they do it, when they do it, and where they do it is up to them." An example Pink cites is the computer software company Meddius. Some people outside the company thought CEO Jeff Gunther was crazy to use ROWE. How can you know what your employees are doing if they're not on site? Pink explains, "But in [Gunther's] view, the team was accomplishing more under this new management. One reason: They were focused on the work itself rather than on whether someone would call them a slacker for leaving at 3:00 pm to watch a daughter's soccer game. For them, it's all about craftsmanship. And they need a lot of autonomy." [1]

Pink could have reached the same conclusions if he studied the NYSAIS staff. It's safe to say the staff is focused intently on the work and appreciates the autonomy. The seven-member staff is both talented and committed—and has not changed in the past five years. Each staff member is a tribute to the success of this service-oriented organization.

Of course, it's not just about the staff. Executive Director Mark Lauria always makes a point of recognizing the hundreds of volunteers who work with the staff to facilitate the proper functioning of the organization. Whether it is through serving on the NYSAIS Board of Trustees, an accreditation visiting committee, or a conference planning committee, or through hosting a workshop at a member school, volunteers provide the added support NYSAIS needs to be a dynamic organization serving the broad needs of its members.

To run an organization in this manner—staff and volunteers spread across a large state—requires serious organizational

NYSAIS STAFF

ANDREW S. COOKE, Assistant Director for Technology and Innovative Strategies (Including: Social Media, Listserves, Newsletter Coordinator)

MARIA FLORES SEIBERT, Administrative Coordinator for Communications and Operations (Including: Exhibitor Showcases)

MARK W. LAURIA, PH.D., Executive Director

JUDITH SHERIDAN, PH.D., Associate Director for Evaluation and Accreditation (Including: Administrator, Experienced Leaders Advising Schools (ELAS))

GEORGE SWAIN, Associate Director for Evaluation and Accreditation (Including: Director, Emerging Leaders Institute (ELI); Director, NYSAIS-*Now*)

Barbara Swanson, Associate Director for Professional Development (Including: Conferences, Workshops, Conference Planning Committees)

Diana Wahrlich, Chief Financial Officer (Including: Finance Committee, Human Resources, Operations, Billing, Refunds)

Front to back: Andrew, Mark, Barbara, George, Maria, Diana, and Judy

skills. It also requires a highly technologically literate staff. While it can be a challenge to physically gather staff together for meetings and planning, they are able to conduct much of the work virtually. Here is what the NYSAIS staff-meeting arrangement looks like today:

> The staff meets in person at the Mohonk Mountain House in New Paltz for conferences and gathers for its annual meeting at the Carey Institute for Global Good in Rensselaerville. The rest of the time, the staff interacts as a group primarily via the Zoom Conferencing platform. [2]

When I spoke to Judy Sheridan, Associate Director for Evaluation and Accreditation, she made a point of saying,

"Using Zoom Conferencing and having a virtual office are a very efficient way for us to work, but we try to balance it with our personal communications and presence. The regional NYSAIS meetings are one manifestation of this commitment. The other is the staff visits to schools. All of us visit schools. It is a very important part of our year to make sure that we are in touch with new heads and school staff. So I think the real benefit of the virtual office has been our awareness of the strengths of the medium as well as our awareness of what we need to do to mitigate its weaknesses. We never want our interactions and relationships with members to be impersonal." [3]

Diana Wahrlich, Chief Financial Officer, added, "The virtual office does save time and money; and those are the two big factors that encourage people to want to continue working for NYSAIS. It is such an awesome advantage for employees. People don't particularly like commuting, especially when there's a lot of traffic. By holding virtual meetings, we are saving the staff lots of time. We are also saving schools the travel expenses we'd otherwise incur."

Sheridan and George Swain, Associate Director for Evaluation and Accreditation, meet often online with regional and state association executives around the country. Barbara Swanson, Associate Director for Professional Development, uses video conferencing on a regular basis to coordinate the work of the numerous conference planning committees.

Of course, one of the most important aspects of establishing and maintaining a virtual office is to also make sure a human is readily available for members when they need to communicate other than through email, voicemail, or other electronic means. We have all experienced the frustration of the limitations of email when trying to solve a problem with, say, a school, bank, or online purchase. You reach a point where you just need to talk with a person. NYSAIS has that person in Maria Flores Seibert, Administrative Coordinator for Communications and Operations. Seibert is, as they say, only a phone call away from members. And when a member calls, he or she will find an optimistic, welcoming voice. Ninety percent of the calls Seibert fields deal with questions about conference or workshop registration that originate on the website. But there are other issues as well: callers needing, say, to get in touch with another staff person or struggling to navigate the NYSAIS website to find specific information. Sometimes Seibert acts as "gatekeeper" to ensure a caller's confidentiality or to provide guidance to a concerned parent about a school issue. Whatever the members' needs, Maria Flores Seibert is there to help, always with an encouraging and optimistic voice.

An area where virtual offices need a good human behind the scenes is when it comes to overseeing organization finances, an area that demands constant attention to detail. In my many interactions with NYSAIS over the past thirty years—as a member, volunteer, trustee, and staff member—I found that when it came to association finances, Diana Wahrlich never let the virtual office get in the way of how she took care of business. She has worked hard to use the technology to keep NYSAIS financially sound.

The goal all around is to leverage technology and people power to their fullest potential.

Still, there is something to be said for in-person meetings, especially staff gatherings. What has become a high point in the life of the NYSAIS staff is the annual residential staff retreat at the Carey Institute for Global Good, a nonprofit center thirty miles southwest of Albany. This time together gives the staff an opportunity to discuss the goals and objectives for the association face to face. Whether reviewing the latest updates in tech-

Andrew Cooke (right) presenting at a staff retreat.

nology, an impending revision of the accreditation manual, an idea for a new institute, or a new way to facilitate conference objectives, the staff can hash out ideas, thoughts, and concerns in a nonvirtual setting that is conducive to reflection. I remember attending a retreat when Andrew Cooke, Associate Director for Technology and Innovative Strategies, was explaining how to maximize the use of the upgraded FileMaker database. With everyone in the room at the same time, he could project his explanation on a screen in real-time. The presentation was clear and seamless. [4]

In Catherine Steiner-Adair's book *The Big Disconnect: Protecting Childhood and Family Relationships in the Digital Age*, she makes an important point regarding real versus virtual communication: "Unfortunately, in ways that matter [technology] is often a model of connection that favors quantity over quality, breadth over depth, and image over intimacy. The tech culture is conditioning us to accept that as an unquestioned norm. And it is training our children to think that way, too." [5]

I want to make it clear that, while the NYSAIS staff uses

technology expediently and has created some virtual programs that serve member schools well (more on this later), the staff is *real* and is dedicated to taking good care of the member schools and the *real* people who work at these schools, caring for and educating their students.

Lauria is very clear about the distinction between real and virtual communication. In a recent article, he notes: "One of the greatest gains in communication has been access. With schools from Buffalo to Albany to New York City, all members are able to easily participate in NYSAIS committees, commissions, and study groups. Face-to-face meetings, while desirable, limit participation to those in closer geographic proximity, especially with shorter meetings."

He also makes it clear that the virtual meetings of today are a vast improvement over the conference calls of past decades. "While telephone calls increased the geographical range of meetings," he says, "active participation was limited because no one could see each other and one was never sure about the actual engagement level of each participant. Additionally, sharing and editing documents was extremely cumbersome and time-consuming." [6]

Lauria will also tell you that the independent school associations across the nation have vastly different work environments from each other. As a result, they have a markedly different ability to deliver services to their members. [7] NYSAIS is committed to its hybrid environment of in-person meetings and events with virtual meetings and programs because the staff believes it's what works best for the independent schools of New York.

As we will see, this arrangement also mirrors the changes in schools themselves—as technology has begun to force us to reevaluate what we mean by "school" today.

CHAPTER TWO

Evolving Member Services

The lifeblood of member organizations is not only the network of members but also the services the organization provides its members. Among the many services provided by independent school associations are accreditation, annual conferences and workshops, access to articles and webinars, job listings, and online resources.

The bottom line is to offer real value for membership dues. During my thirty-year relationship with NYSAIS, I have been most proud to be a part of the services and support it has provided to member schools, and the opportunity to volunteer with NYSAIS to help it be the best state association in the independent school world.

I address accreditation and professional development opportunities in separate chapters. Here, I focus on the other essential services NYSAIS provides its members and the evolution of those services in recent years.

Communication

Undoubtedly, the easiest and quickest way to communicate with NYSAIS is through its website. There, members will find workshop and conference information and registration; career opportunities; large resource libraries for administrators, teachers, and parents, including video, livestream, interviews, webinars, and support programs for schools; and much more. The NYSAIS website is a robust resource for all schools and anyone who wants to learn more about the association and its mission.

Through its online newsletter, *What's Happening @ NYSAIS*, NYSAIS also lets members know about current and upcoming services and events.

An online issue of *What's Happening @ NYSAIS*

Here is a perfect example, taken from the April 2017 issue of *What's Happening*:

> Innovation and global connections were two of the main themes of the recent OESIS-CERNET Conference in Beijing that Mark Lauria, Barbara Swanson, Judy Sheridan, and George Swain attended along with educators from around the United States and China. Each of the members of the NYSAIS delegation presented conference sessions on themes related to innovations that NYSAIS has been championing in both professional development and accreditation. In addition, Mark, Barbara, Judy, and George visited several innovative schools and met with a range of educational leaders and policy experts to develop a more sophisticated understanding of the educational landscape in China today. [1]

Regional Meetings

Each year, NYSAIS hosts regional meetings throughout the state. These meetings are hosted by member schools in the following areas: Hudson Valley, Buffalo, Rochester, Long Island, Capitol Region, Brooklyn, New York City, and Westchester County, The meetings offer an opportunity for schools to ask staff members questions and listen to them talk about new developments and program updates. Most impressive is the growth in popularity of these events. As Mark Lauria points out, the school participation in regional meetings has grown considerably "from 2009, when 77 schools attended these meetings, to 2016, when 118 schools attended the meetings." [2]

One of the best byproducts of these meetings, though, is the professional networking for the members.

Today's Goals

➢ **Meet new NYSAIS members**
➢ **NYSAIS and Hybrid Learning Consortium Partnership**
➢ **Discuss NYSAIS services:**
  – ELAS
  – NYSAIS *Now*
  – Listservs
  – Website
  – NYSAIS Conferences and Workshops
  – China Educational Opportunity
➢ **NYSAIS Accreditation**
  – Accreditation Update
  – DASL and Accreditation Statistics for Benchmarks
➢ **Regional Discussion Forum**

A typical regional meeting agenda

School Advice and Support

The availability and use of institutional counseling through the NYSAIS office and services are remarkable. Working in school consulting and administering the Experienced Leaders Advising Schools (ELAS) program gave me new perspective on how important it is for school heads and board chairs to have access to a knowledgeable outside resource. When schools are struggling with leadership transitions, governance issues, finance challenges, etc., heads and board chairs can always contact the NYSAIS office and get pointed in the right direction for advice and counsel.

Hybrid Learning

One of the newest services NYSAIS provides its members is the Hybrid Learning Consortium. The consortium, which began in the 2015-2016 school year, allows member schools to implement an online learning program as part of their current curricula.

This partnership will benefit schools by:

- allowing them to expand their current course offerings;
- providing them with an online curricular presence at a highly competitive rate;
- connecting faculty and students with faculty and students in a growing collaborative of schools throughout the world; and
- assisting faculty at NYSAIS schools in developing the expertise needed to create and teach online synchronous and asynchronous courses. [3]

Experienced Leaders Advising Schools (ELAS)

This is another fairly new program, begun in 2012, proving to be invaluable to school leaders. The program's mission is to, "provide low-cost, high-impact advising and mentoring for leadership and governance." [4]

Under the direction of ELAS administrator Judy Sheridan, here is how the program supports schools:

- ELAS consultants, referred to as "ed-visors," include retired heads of school and senior administrators with significant experience and expertise in independent schools.
- Ed-visors are trained in organizational consulting and mentoring and are rigorously assessed for efficacy to ensure consistency among advising engagements, called ed-visements.

- As in the best independent schools, ELAS does not use a boilerplate, one-size-fits-all approach. Built upon a solid foundation of best practices combined with current research, each ed-visement is custom-designed to meet the specific needs of each educational community.

To date, more than 25 member schools have taken advantage of the ELAS program. With its current 12-member ed-visor roster, ed-visements have included:

- board professional development—including retreats; governance, leadership, and head support; and bylaws/policy review and implementation;
- financial planning, projections, policy development, and financial aid;
- strategic planning;
- fund-raising strategies;
- executive coaching;
- enrollment strategizing;
- classroom/grade expansion; and
- personnel management and compensation models.

Best Practices

NYSAIS offers its members detailed lists of best practices for highly practical reasons. As the NYSAIS Board of Trustees puts it, "Experience indicates that when [best practices] are followed schools benefit and when they are not followed it is to the detriment of the individuals and institutions involved. Open and forthright communication is critical within the context of appropriate and thoughtful expectations of all involved."

In short, schools function best when they follow best practices. NYSAIS offers its members best practices in the following areas:

- Admissions
- Athletics
- Equity & Justice
- School Governance
- Heads and the Search Process
- Hiring of Faculty and Staff
- Professional Development [5]

Seminars and Roundtable Discussions

Offered on a regular basis, NYSAIS Seminars and Roundtable Discussions bring heads of school and trustees together to share concerns and programmatic successes. Among the topics offered and discussed are finances, care for the head of school, governance issues, and leadership transitions.

Business Affairs Council (BAC)

Extremely active, the BAC, a group of business managers from NYSAIS schools, is the volunteer business "think tank" that utilizes some of the best financial minds in the NYSAIS community to solve school business problems and provide innovative solutions. Among other things, the BAC has been active in helping to create several NYSAIS consortiums. In fact, in order to gain more flexibility in its IRS 501(c)3 status, NYSAIS, in February 2011, established NYSAIS Operations, Inc., a 501(c)6 trade association. In 2011-2012, a BAC subcommittee formed the healthcare consortium that works through NYSAIS Operations, Inc.

Here are some facts about the healthcare consortium:

- As of 2016-2017, 18 schools have joined the consortium, covering 2,500 people.
- The average rate increase, except for one year, has been significantly under the average for all NYSAIS schools.
- The consortium represents approximately $26,000,000 worth of insurance coverage, which allows the consortium to better negotiate rates.
- The consortium has saved the participating schools millions of dollars since its inception.
- Services have expanded beyond medical insurance to include a Human Resources/eCompliance Program, eServices, Wellness, and COBRA administration.
- The consortium is governed by the Health Insurance Program Advisory Committee (HIPAC), which is composed of both heads of school and business managers. [6]

The BAC has also created a purchasing consortium, working with W.B. Mason, an office products retailer. Further, the BAC is instrumental in planning the annual business officers conference at the Mohonk Mountain House in New Paltz.

State Political Presence and Monitoring

The founding members of NYSAIS were very clear about the association's purpose regarding state governance and regulations. "The purpose of the organization shall be to promote the independence and well-being of and public regard for the independent schools of the State of New York; to safeguard the interests of these schools in the matter of legislation and regulation; to foster mutually beneficial relations with the New York State Education Department and other educational agencies...." [7]

Due to revolving state politics and legislation, NYSAIS, as an IRS 501(c)3 nonprofit organization, found that it could no longer advocate for its member schools through lobbying and political financial support. This advocacy has been an important part of the work and service NYSAIS provides its member schools. One example is the work NYSAIS has done over the years to help New York State independent schools receive state financial support for busing and educational services such as library funds and special education support for students. Now, under the new 501(c)6 entity, NYSAIS has more flexibility regarding advocacy and can continue to lobby and support those politicians who support NYSAIS goals and political interests.

Future Services

So much of the desired service NYSAIS provides its members comes from members themselves—whether through the staff listening to members at regional meetings, NYSAIS professional development events, and accreditation committee meetings, or the through the NYSAIS Board of Trustees. These are the voices that speak on behalf of the member schools. Their willingness to contribute their ideas, along with the NYSAIS staff eagerness to listen, is a large part of why NYSAIS has served so admirably its nearly 200 member schools for the past 70 years—and why it continues to evolve so well with the times.

ACCREDITED BY

NYSAIS

NEW YORK STATE ASSOCIATION OF INDEPENDENT SCHOOLS

Manual for Evaluation and Accreditation

**For NYSAIS Accreditation visits in the
2017-2018, 2018-2019 school years.**

Mark W. Lauria, Ph.D.
Executive Director

Judith Sheridan, Ph.D.
Associate Director for Evaluation and Accreditation

George Swain
Associate Director for Evaluation and Accreditation

Version 4.0
Approved by the NYSAIS Commission on Accreditation, May 2016

Cover of the NYSAIS Accreditation Manual. Complete manual is available at www.nysais.org.

CHAPTER THREE

Strengthening Schools Through Accreditation

Mark Lauria painted a beautiful portrait of New York independent schools in an article published in *The Parents League of New York Review 2016*. "Over the last three centuries," he writes, "New York independent schools have provided a rich tapestry of educational opportunities. Some of these schools are described as traditional or progressive; others promote specialized curriculums designed around a particular pedagogy, such as Montessori or Waldorf. There are single-gender schools, religious schools, day schools, boarding schools, and schools that serve the needs of special education students. Each school provides a different path for students to reach their destination; within the panoply of independent schools, parents will likely find several in which their child will be educated in the way that she or he learns best." [1]

How does a school know if it is a good school? How does it define "good"? What is it that sets one school apart from another? Is a school using its endowment for the right purposes? Is it managing its leadership transition well? Is it time to rethink the curriculum or stay the course? Is the school meeting its mission? Addressing these and other key questions is where accreditation comes into the equation.

Schools often dread the periodic accreditation process because it demands work and some soul-searching. But when the process is done right, schools come out stronger for it—with a clearer sense of who they are.

Judy Sheridan was especially eloquent when she stated in her recent *Independent School* article "Accreditation has become even more important than in the past. Why? Because, when understood, accreditation inspires confidence that independent schools, as varied as they are, remain a true 'value proposition.' Furthermore, for the schools themselves, the accreditation process is critical in understanding not just who they are but where they are going. In other words, the process helps schools not only to survive, but also to lead the way in transforming education for our changing times." [2]

Lois Bailey, who single-handedly took care of all of NYSAIS school accreditations for 25 years, was responsible for defining and refining the accreditation process and implementing the criteria and standards all member schools must meet for accreditation, keeping in mind that the New York State Board of Regents required specific standards that also met the New York State Department of Education standards. Indeed, Bailey's work led to a major change in the accreditation process in 2011.

The NYSAIS Commission on Accreditation made a decision to require that all member schools be accredited by NYSAIS. Prior to that, schools could choose to be accredited by NYSAIS or the Middle States Association. This change increased the number of schools that NYSAIS would accredit each year and was a significant factor in the need to add two Associate Directors for Accreditation and Evaluation to the NYSAIS staff.

When Bailey retired in 2013, Sheridan, having worked as an administrator and teacher at the Dalton School and being active in both NYSAIS and NAIS as a presenter and workshop facilitator, learned the steps and procedures it took to work through all of the accreditation procedures Bailey established. Lauria quickly realized, however, that if the new standards of accreditation were going to survive and grow—especially if the accreditation process was going to meet the demands to ensure quality governance, finances, and technology—NYSAIS would need a second staff person to help Sheridan. That person turned out to be George Swain.

Working at Poughkeepsie Day School and as a long-time volunteer to NYSAIS, Swain was deeply involved in the Beginning Teachers Institute, ongoing professional development sessions, and the burgeoning Emerging Leaders Institute. After joining NYSAIS, he and Sheridan have accomplished a great deal to strengthen the accreditation process.

Specifically, they:

- published the new and improved *Manual for Evaluation and Accreditation Manual, Version 4.0*;
- streamlined the accreditation process—both decennial and five-year reviews—to better accommodate the many volunteers it takes to perform school accreditations, evaluations, visits, and reports;
- through the implementation of video conferencing, established a system so the statewide Commission on Accreditation can meet regularly and efficiently; and
- refined and expanded the use of synchronous and asynchronous online collaboration tools to ensure

that the work of accreditation is as efficient and effective as possible.

What is most remarkable in all of this work, though, is that while the accreditation program was being strengthened by Sheridan and Swain, Swain was administering the Emerging Leaders Institute program with Marcy Mann, Associate Head for Academic Affairs at the Professional Children's School in Manhattan, and taking an instrumental role in building the technology infrastructure with Andrew Cooke to make NYSAIS-*Now* the vibrant resource it is today. For her part, Sheridan stepped up to take over the administration of the Experienced Leaders Advising Schools (ELAS) program when the former director (that would be me) decided to move closer to retirement. This multitasking is a perfect example of how the NYSAIS staff works. One of Sheridan's and Swain's most important responsibilities is to coordinate the work of the 20 dedicated members of the Commission on Accreditation. Not surprisingly, all of the members of the commission are volunteers. Reading all of the school self-studies and the subsequent visiting committee reports is a monumental task, especially when commissioners have a full-time job of leading schools.

Manual for Evaluation and Accreditation

Over the past three years, as noted, Sheridan and Swain, in partnership with the Commission on Accreditation, did an extensive review and revision of the *Manual for Evaluation and Accreditation.* Here is some of the thinking and the approach used to make this latest version, 4.0, stronger than earlier versions:

- The review included NYSAIS staff and an extensive collaboration with the Commission on Accreditation.

- The review team put less emphasis on the departmental examination of the school and more emphasis on a global program review. The whole manual was reviewed at once rather than in segments.
- The team looked carefully for redundancy and inefficiencies in the old manual, condensing the number of sections from 11 to 7.
- The process began with criteria to drive categories to get commission buy-in, then evolved to develop questions to guide the school's self-study.
- One example of making the manual and process more efficient was to combine pedagogy practices with professional development practices.

It is interesting to look at the layout and content of accreditation manuals over the past decade—and what the changes tell us about the shift in focus.

The underlying reasoning behind the latest revision of the accreditation manual is to:

- further emphasize analysis and encourage strategic thinking;
- prioritize Teaching and Learning by placing this section second following Mission and Culture, rather than fifth as in the previous manual;
- promote a holistic approach to Teaching and Learning by discouraging an approach that separates the educational program into disciplines and divisions;
- simplify and encourage access and use of quantitative data by providing an enriched database through a collaboration with NAIS and its Data and Analysis for

History of the *Manual for Evaluation and Accreditation*

Section	2006 Edition	3.0 (February 2011)	4.0 (May 2016)
One	Purposes and Objectives	Mission and Culture	Mission and Culture
Two	School Culture, Community, and Staff	Governance	Teaching and Learning
Three	Program	School Operations, Finance, and Advancement	Governance
Four	Governance	Admissions and Financial Assistance	Financial Sustainability
Five	Administration	Educational Program	Operations
Six	Conclusion (commentary on the findings and future)	Students and Student Services	Community
Seven		Faculty, Administrators, and Non-teaching Personnel	Self-Study Process, Reflection and Conclusion
Eight		Parents	
Nine		The School in Its Community	
Ten		Internal and External Communication	
Eleven		Conclusion: Process and Reflection	

School Leadership (DASL) database and using a one-button approach to generating reports;

• revise the criteria into logical units: baseline criteria and strategic criteria (which schools can rate on a scale of 1 to 6). This allows schools and the visiting committees to focus on strategic and generative issues;

• eliminate repetition and redundancies, which resulted in a reduction of the number of sections and the number of criteria for accreditation; and

• ensure that schools adhere to state and local laws and regulations by having the board chair and head of school verify a list of compliance statements prior to the visit.

As part of the overall accreditation design, an exciting new project is being developed. It examines all of the accreditation ratings—by committee and by school—using a new FileMaker database developed by staff member Andrew Cooke. The database examines average ratings in each chapter, standard deviations, and even compares (anonymously) committees with the average ratings versus length of accreditation stipulations.

Accreditation Visits

In any given year, NYSAIS undertakes roughly 35 to 40 school accreditation visits, with half being decennial (ten-year) accreditations and half being five-year review accreditations. Decennial visits are accomplished in a four-day visit to the school, and depending on the size of the school, roughly five- to fourteen-member, all-volunteer teams comprise the visiting committee. Five-year review visits are accomplished in a two-day visit to the school with three-member teams. Accordingly, with the support of the Commission on Accreditation, Sheridan and Swain have been working hard to establish the size of decennial committees without diminishing the quality in order to lessen the demand on volunteers; increase the efficiency of the process; and reduce school expenses, which are necessary to accommodate visiting committees.

Commission on Accreditation

The overall guidance, direction, and responsibility for the accreditation process rest with the Commission on Accreditation. This group of twenty dedicated volunteers, all of whom are heads of school, read the accreditation reports, and with the chair of the visiting committee and guidance from Sheridan and Swain, make the decision on whether schools meet the criteria for accreditation. Enhanced by video conferencing, a subcommittee of the commission meets to discuss the reports and accreditation documents with the chair of the visiting committee.

The head of the subcommittee makes a recommendation regarding the term of accreditation to the full commission. This is where Zoom conferencing and NAIS's database, DASL, have made a significant difference in making this process less time-consuming and more efficient, and enables the commission to have a generative and strategic discussion on each accreditation and in the long run build a better accreditation program.

Ultimately, it is the commission that makes accreditation recommendations to the NYSAIS Board of Trustees on whether the association will grant accreditation or not. This is probably one of the most vital aspects of NYSAIS.

You will find that school accreditation standards are an integral part of school quality assurance throughout the independent school community. It is important to note that state and regional associations, along with holding their schools accountable, hold themselves accountable as well. Lauria, as NYSAIS Executive Director, and Sheridan, fulfilling a three-year rotation as one of three Directors of Accreditation, serve on the NAIS Commission on Accreditation. They both represent NYSAIS as members of the NAIS Commission on Accreditation and both have been closely involved in the NAIS commission's own self-study process for the purpose of association quality assurance and improvement.

As noted on the NAIS website, "the NAIS Commission on Accreditation was established by the NAIS Board of Trustees in 2001 at the request of accrediting independent school state and regional associations, and convened for the first time in 2002. The commission's work is intended to assure the quality of independent school accrediting programs."

A key responsibility of the commission is to develop a public understanding of the value and purpose of state and regional independent school accrediting programs. In addition, the commission:

- develops criteria for effective independent school accreditation practices, exemplary standards, and models of successful accreditation policies and procedures; and
- engages in research to inform accreditation practice. [3]

In her *Independent School* article, Sheridan made it clear that accreditation today is not about rubber-stamping an existing program. It's about re-evaluating a school program in a 21st-century context. "The amalgam of considerations and evaluations, which define the accreditation process," she writes, "becomes a force that leads to change, at times to 'disruption,' and often to innovative, strategic initiatives that better educate our children and prepare them for a dynamic future." [4]

The NYSAIS staff understands this link between accreditation and institutional growth as well as any organization, and has displayed a deep commitment to leveraging the accreditation process for educational excellence in every member school.

Here is what the NYSAIS channel looks like on the YouTube.

CHAPTER FOUR

Technology and the Future of Schools

Barbara Swanson was hired as a NYSAIS part-time associate in 1984. That year, she remembers attending a meeting of the Business Affairs Council at Friends Seminary in New York City when the talk turned to a newfangled contraption. Someone said, "Does anybody here have a fax machine?" A few people said they did, so the person who asked the question then asked, "Well, what do you use it for? I can't figure it out. The board thinks we should have one, but I don't know why we need one." [1]

Fax machines, of course, would soon be in just about every school and business. They are still viable means of communication today, but very few people use them because these once remarkable devices are now seen as slow, cumbersome, and borderline obsolete. The development of digital technology in business, society, and education between 1984 and the present is almost hard to fathom. What is clear is that technology's omnipresence today has changed so much of the way we live—

from the way we communicate, to the way we get our news and entertainment, to the way we shop, and, yes, to the way we work and learn.

Today, new technologies arrive at a dizzying pace—from the increasingly sophisticated laptops, smart phones, and tablets, to the growing number of powerful software programs, to the increasing speeds with which we can access the Internet. By all reports, it won't be long before we all have self-driving cars. Full-fledged AI (Artificial Intelligence) might not be far behind.

In this landscape, schools everywhere wrestle with how best to use technology in the classroom and to support their programs. Some ed-tech companies are even using technology to challenge our understanding of what a school is. With Khan Academy and its ilk, do we even need classrooms?

The technology revolution, of course, has impacted organizations such as NYSAIS, too. Over the past several years, much of the job of navigating and implementing technology at NYSAIS has come under the leadership and expertise of staff member Andrew Cooke, Assistant Director for Technology and Innovative Strategies. I explain some of these innovations in the context of their usage in other sections of this book (e.g., professional development via the Internet, online registrations for conferences and workshops, etc.). Here, I examine how technology has impacted much of NYSAIS's core work with members.

For NYSAIS, a significant part of the overall technology design to date has been to:

- expand conference offerings to schools located upstate that could not always send teachers and administrators to events at Mohonk Mountain House or the New York City area where the majority of member schools are located;

- offer livestreaming through NYSAIS *NOW*, the organization's vibrant online site for professional development and school improvement resources;
- better connect schools across the state via high-quality, Internet-based professional development offerings;
- support and enhance the virtual office (discussed in Chapter I); and
- provide a database that supplies congruous data regardless of where the staff members are located.

Personal Connection and Smart Data

Much of the technology that NYSAIS uses is fairly typical of most organizations today. For instance, staff members use Facebook and Twitter and other social media as vehicles for communication that provide valuable resources to its followers and create a sense of community.

As for Twitter, Mark Lauria leads the way, as of May 1, 2017, with 5,607 tweets and 1,768 followers. George Swain is alongside him with 6,270 tweets and 1,237 followers. The organization itself has 2,039 Twitter followers.

NYSAIS, as noted, also has a robust database that staff members can access and update remotely. End-users don't see all of the work that goes into building and tweaking an organi-

NYSAIS
The New York State Association of Independent Schools promotes the independence, well-being and public understanding of, and respect for, New York independe...
livestream.com

zation's website, technology infrastructure, and database. Like other organizations, NYSAIS works daily to update its technology to keep its programs and services running as seamlessly as possible. But it does take a great deal of effort.

A perfect example is the way Cooke has built and managed the NYSAIS database. NYSAIS's first database management program, Panorama, served its purpose for a while. But on NYSAIS's behalf, Cooke eventually replaced it with a customized, fully integrated database using Apple's FileMaker platform.

"One of the things that I love most about FileMaker," Cooke points out, "is the ease in implementing new technologies. If we had to create interfaces to the database for Mac, Windows, cloud/browser, and iPhone, we would struggle to do it or keep up over time. With FileMaker, the interfaces are built into the platform, enabling nonprofits like us to leverage their technology to offer something we couldn't on our own. It makes my job easier and keeps NYSAIS at the forefront of technology and innovation among our association peers." [2]

Lauria concurs. "The system allows us to connect via any platform," he says. "After a school visit, we can log into our notes, which go right into the database. And everybody has instant access to it all. The database is now also used to track accreditation visiting committee effectiveness and efficiency, which saves schools money and helps with volunteer support." [3]

The data that affect school membership—such as program registrations, accreditation information, and school visits by staff—are stored in a central database that can be viewed and updated by the staff wherever they are located, and on virtually any device. Today, thanks to NAIS and NYSAIS, members can view their own data and compare it with other NYSAIS member schools, it also enables them to benchmark their data nationally.

In years past, finding and accessing such data was an immensely time-consuming and complicated process. Today, thanks to NYSAIS, members can:

- benchmark their individual data against other schools locally, statewide, and nationally;
- survey the school community—including parents, alumni, board, and applicants;
- review and recruit top talent, keeping track of salary and compensation data;
- ensure healthy enrollment through demographics and community outreach;
- support their boards of trustees through improved reports; and
- track how their schools have performed over any given period of time. [4]

Quality Online Programming

Beyond social media and the gathering and leveraging of data for school support and improvement, NYSAIS uses technology to deliver quality programming. In the early days of electronic meetings, the technology was more than a bit sketchy. But Cooke points out that NYSAIS's eSeminars and the virtual trustee and head of school roundtable discussions today are very reliable and personable. [5] Improvements in bandwidth and software have improved the reliability, picture quality, and ease of connectivity.

One of the major enhancements at NYSAIS was the introduction of NYSAIS *NOW* in the summer of 2014. Because this online service is so pervasive in the NYSAIS community today, I discuss what it offers in this chapter and other chapters, particularly in the chapter on professional development. I believe

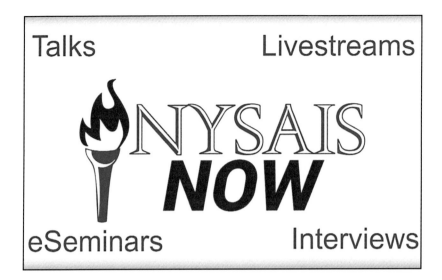

that NYSAIS *NOW*'s most important value is the way it gives both its member schools and the field of education, in general, access to high-quality, on-point programming.

One example is an eSeminar, "Caring for Your Head" that I did for NYSAIS trustees in November 2015. We had a good number of trustees who tuned in live. But I was also able to share the seminar later with school trustees who were not able to tune in at the time. My presentation was just one of many available through NYSAIS *NOW*. The site covers a broad range of topics, with a particular focus on school leadership and governance. Other eSeminars include Debra Wilson (issues that keep independent school leaders up at night), Reveta Bowers (on fund-raising and endowments), and Sarah Hofstra (online learning). Among the interviews are insightful conversations with Ali Michael (on racial identity development), Tim Burns (on brain science and learning), Pat Bassett (big shifts in education), and Tristan Harris (on technology and ethics). Among the recorded talks are presentations from Andrew Solomon (on identity development and support), Dave Mochel (on finding balance amid the demands and distractions of school life), and Emily Pilloton (on how design thinking can transform schools).

With its growing library of valuable video offerings, NYSAIS *NOW* has its own YouTube channel. Through YouTube, NYSAIS is able to share its video productions with anyone wanting to improve his or her understanding of education and leadership skills.

Whenever you see the NYSAIS livestream logo next to a presentation on the NYSAIS website, you know you will be given the opportunity to watch the event live no matter where you are. In some cases, you will be able to stream the presentation after it has been presented live. I better understood that value of both options when I could not make it to NYSAIS's 2016 Conference for Heads of School. Although I was unable to attend in person, I wanted to see and hear the keynote speaker, *New York Times* columnist Frank Bruni. Through NYSAIS *NOW*, I got to do just that, watching and listening through livestreaming right in my own living room. It was so powerful—seeing it live at the same time as my colleagues. What Bruni discussed was also encapsulated in his latest book, *Where You Go Is Not Who You'll Be*. After watching the livestream, I immediately went to the library and checked out a copy of the book, read it in a week, and began referencing it in my own talks.

A significant piece of NYSAIS *NOW*, livestreams allow you

Here is how livestreams are presented on the NYSAIS website.

to experience selected talks by keynote conference speakers in real-time throughout the year. Attend one (or all) of our outstanding NYSAIS residential conferences without leaving the comfort of your home or office. No registration is required. Simply set aside the time and go to the NYSAIS *NOW* livestream page at *livestream.com/nysaislive* to participate. To find out more about specific talks and speakers, please consult the full conference program at *nysais.org*. Additional NYSAIS *NOW* livestream sessions will be announced throughout the year. [6]

Lauria points out that the steady improvements in technology have led to the ever-improving quality of these livestreams. "If you look at our early livestreams," he notes, "the quality wasn't great. But we were learning. Under Andrew's guidance, the visual quality of each livestream is now really very professional. The way he edits the events also makes them look like studio productions. If you listen to the first interviews we did and then listen to the newer interviews, there's quite a big difference." [7]

Cooke adds, "Over the last four years, a number of people from schools in other states have either attended our conferences or participated via livestream or YouTube. We get comments all the time saying that there is nothing like this in their associations." [8]

In the end, NYSAIS is fortunate to have the technology leadership, facilitation, and expertise of Cooke. With it, the organization is able to leverage technology in service to schools. I believe Lauria describes NYSAIS embrace and use of technology the best. "As educators, we talk about 21st-century skills," he says, "but even experienced educators feel they are behind the technology curve with students. NYSAIS, through the use of video collaboration technology, has provided countless administrators and teachers with authentic professional development.

As they have used this technology to support their administrative work, many have begun to see the possibilities in the classroom. This leads to an obvious question: If we are serious about leading our schools and students into the world of their future, why would we continuing to use legacy technology that became popular when cars had fins and AM radios? For many educational leaders in NYSAIS, it is hard to imagine returning to a pre-video collaboration work environment." [9]

MULTIPLE GENERATIONS @ WORK

Five Generations Working Side by Side in 2020

TRADITIONALISTS Born 1900-1945	BOOMERS Born 1946-1964	GEN X Born 1965-1976	MILLENNIAL Born 1977-1997	GEN 2020 After 1997
Great Depression	Vietnam, Moon Landing	Fall of Berlin Wall	9/11 Attacks	Age 15 and Younger
World War II	Civil/Women's Rights	Gulf War	Community Service	Optimistic
Disciplined	Experimental	Independent	Immediacy	High Expectations
Workplace Loyalty	Innovators	Free Agents	Confident, Diversity	Apps
Move to the 'Burbs	Hard Working	Internet, MTV, AIDS	Social Everything	Social Games
Vaccines	Personal Computer	Mobile Phone	Google, Facebook	Tablet Devices

CHAPTER FIVE

Professional Development

I was a firsthand witness to the development—no, "explosion" is a better word—of NYSAIS professional development program. My observation began in 1986, when I first met Fred Calder, then NYSAIS's newly appointed executive director. At the time, I was working at East Woods School on the North Shore of Long Island. Calder was visiting the school as part of his first year of getting acquainted with the schools he would be leading at the state level. We met in the school library—and I was impressed by his knowledge of education and vision for the association.

Soon thereafter, I was asked to join the NYSAIS Professional Development Committee. That is where I met Barbara Swanson, who at the time was in her third year as the NYSAIS staff person in charge of coordinating professional development activities for member schools. I also met Gordon Clem, then head of St. Thomas Choir School in Manhattan, who taught me and others all we needed to know about the commitment NYSAIS devotes to professional development for its members.

Eventually, I would become the chair of the committee, which gave me the opportunity to work even closer with Swanson and to see the magic she performed daily, building the professional development program to what it is today. She and the committee collaborated much the way a head of school and the board of trustees would. One of Swanson's great leadership qualities is that she will never dismiss an idea out of hand. The proof of this is in the revenue NYSAIS's professional development offerings have generated over the years. Clearly, the membership has the desire for and appreciation of the varied programs NYSAIS makes available each year. This chapter will illuminate many of those professional opportunities.

The Generational Challenge

One of the challenges in offering professional development today is that each of the generations currently working in the field of education, not to mention the students themselves, have different comfort levels and interests in technology.

Not all professional development in education focuses on technology, of course, but an increasingly high percentage of it does—either as the delivery system for an event or as the subject itself. As noted in the previous chapter, NYSAIS models the use of technology in its operations and offerings—its resources, services, seminars, conferences, etc. It also knows it needs to offer schools professional development on the use of technology in education—how technology can support the curriculum and also reshape it.

The challenge in doing this is to keep in mind the ways each generation embraces and uses technology.

Indeed, with five generations interacting, it is helpful to

note that Millennials, with 75.4 million, now out-number Baby Boomers. [1] It is also interesting to note that, according to AARP, "the baby boom has become the grandparent boom: There are now more grandparents in the U.S. than ever before—some 70 million, according to the latest census. That's a 24 percent increase since 2001. In fact, of all adults over 30, more than 1 in 3 were grandparents of 2014." [2]

To keep track of the current complex mix of generations and what it means for an organization serving their professional needs, it might be helpful to list the birth years for each:

- iGen, Gen Z, or Centennials—born 1996 and later.
- Millennials or Gen Y—born 1977 to 1995.
- Generation X—born 1965 to 1976.
- Baby Boomers—born 1946 to 1964.
- Greatest, Traditionalists, or Silent Generation— born 1945 and before. [3]

There are no clear lines here, just generational tendencies. For NYSAIS, serving educators from all five generations means that it must be aware of these tendencies and design its professional development programs to reach the broadest range. Another way to put this is that technology and professional development are not synonymous—which is why this chapter is not a subsection of the previous chapter. Professional development today is a complex mix of in-person and virtual offerings. As we will also see, it involves high-quality print material, too.

Internships, Writing, Experiential Learning, and Volunteer Opportunities

NYSAIS has always advocated for educators to be lifelong learners. Doing so pays dividends threefold: strengthens self and career; provides a model for the students; and strengthens the work we do as teachers, mentors, and educators.

In my life as a professional educator, I have tried to take this three-part perspective to heart. The best nonconference/ workshop experiences I have had in the NYSAIS community include serving on accreditation visiting committees; engaging in volunteer opportunities at my school and for NYSAIS; presenting at conferences, institutes, and workshops; and writing articles for various educational publications such as *Independent Teacher*, *Independent School*, *Montessori Life*, and *NYSAIS Professional Development Exchange*.

Regarding the last publication, it was in the fall of 1989 when the NYSAIS Professional Development Committee created the *NYSAIS Professional Development Exchange*, "a newsletter with the purpose of providing NYSAIS independent schools with a forum for exchanging ideas and professional information." [4] At the time, it was the first of its kind to serve a state association of independent schools. While the newsletter did not have a long run, it set the stage for more interschool communication by acting as a catalyst for further discussion and interaction among member schools.

Sometimes it's not easy to see how these opportunities connect. But in my experience, the threads always reveal themselves. For example, an early issue of the newsletter included a survey of member school faculty members, asking them to submit titles of their all-time favorite books. In a subsequent issue, it shared the list. What caught my attention was the overwhelming number of readers who said *A Prayer for Owen Meany* by John Irving was their favorite novel. I had never read it and was inspired to do so immediately. Long story short, it became a favorite of mine as well, and in the fall of 1993, I submitted an article to *Independent School* titled "Meeting Owen Meany."

NYSAIS

Professional   Development   Exchange

Fall   1989

After it was accepted and printed, I received a hand-written note from John Irving—a longtime independent school person himself—saying, "I read with pleasure your 'Meeting Owen Meany' essay in NAIS magazine. Thank you for writing it."

Engagement leads to knowledge; knowledge leads to connection; connection leads to professional growth. This is what NYSAIS understands. Today, if you go on the NYSAIS website, you will find the following request: "The Big Read! What are you reading? Please contribute to this list by writing to Barbara Swanson." It's followed by a sampling of contemporary books recommended by the NYSAIS staff and teachers and administrators of member schools:

Nonfiction

- *Quiet: The Power of Introverts in a World That Can't Stop Talking* by Susan Cain
- *Now You See It: How the Brain Science of Attention Will Transform the Way We Live, Work, and Learn* by Cathy Davidson
- *Reality Is Broken: Why Games Make Us Better and How They Can Change the World* by Jane McGonigal
- *What Would Google Do?* by Jeff Jarvis
- *Brain Rules: 12 Principles for Surviving and Thriving at Work, Home, and School* by John Medina
- *Where Good Ideas Come From: The Natural History of Innovation* by Steven Johnson
- *The Boys in the Boat: Nine Americans and Their*

Epic Quest for Gold at the 1936 Berlin Olympics by Daniel James Brown

Fiction

- *American Wife* by Curtis Sittenfeld
- *Out Stealing Horses* by Per Petterson, translated by Anne Born
- *On Chesil Beach* by Ian McEwan
- *A Prayer for Owen Meany* by John Irving [5]

In an era in which we spend so much time in front of our computers, it is good to be reminded of the value and power of good literature. Professional development is often a matter of a good book and comfortable chair. I might argue that our humanity and professional acuity depend on it.

Conferences and Institutes

Speaking of lists—here's a sample of the many conferences and institutes that NYSAIS hosts annually (with the year they started):

JULY
- Advisory and Service Learning Institute (2012)

AUGUST
- STEAM (Science, Technology, Engineering, Arts, and Mathematics) Camp (2013)
- Summer Residency in Successful Classroom Management (2000)

OCTOBER
- Two Beginning Teachers institutes (1984)

- Special Education Conference (in early stages)
- Counselors and Health Educators Conference (2014)

NOVEMBER
- Conference for Heads of School (1950)
- Assistant Heads and Division Heads Conference (1987)
- Department Chairs Conference (2014)
- After School Conference (2012)

JANUARY
- Sex, Gender, and Sexuality (2012)
- Leaf & Pen: Writing Retreat for Educators (2015)
- Education and Information Technology Conference (1997)

FEBRUARY
- Experienced Teachers Institute (1995)

MARCH
- Brain Conference (2011)
- Institutional Advancement Conference (2007)

APRIL
- Global Language and Culture Conference (2015)
- Admissions and Placement Directors Conference (2002)

MAY
- Athletics Directors Conference (1994)
- Business Affairs Conference (1994)

- College Counselors Conference (2015)
- Diversity Practitioners Conference (2013)

JUNE
- The Office: Conference for Administrative Professionals (2014)
- Early Childhood and Lower School Heads Conference (2007)

The longest-running conference, the Conference for Heads of School, held the first week in November, has established its home at the Mohonk Mountain House in New Paltz since 1978. There is a custom now that every third year NYSAIS heads invite the heads of school from the New Jersey and Connecticut state associations to join them in a regional conversation.

For me, one of the most memorable Conference for Heads of School was in 2011. Focused on the "Music Paradigm," the conference featured maestro Roger Nierenberg as keynote speaker. The maestro along with 32 musicians—with whom he had never worked before—performed for the assembled heads, demonstrating the similarities between being a conductor of an orchestra and being a head of school. As reported in *Symphony* magazine "[Nierenberg's] goal is to help these executives discover basic truths about the functioning of an organization—concepts of leadership, teamwork, and personal empowerment—while simultaneously inspiring them with the music." [6]

Cleverly, the audience was mixed in with the orchestra members, and as the heads of school listened to Tchaikovsky's *Serenade for Strings in C Major, Op. 48*, the maestro eloquently explained the leadership similarities and used audience members to come on stage to conduct the chamber orchestra. When the program concluded, the maestro and orchestra received a long, appreciative standing ovation. [7]

This is just one example of the creative and artful approach NYSAIS takes to engage its members in exploration of school leadership and institutional excellence.

Institutes

I include some NYSAIS's institutes on the list above. But I want to highlight a few here that are particularly important to professional lives of teachers. As NYSAIS notes on its website, the organization "has a longstanding tradition of offering professional support to teachers through the Beginning Teacher Institute (BTI) and the Experienced Teacher Institute (ETI). Each of these institutes, staffed by experienced volunteers, is open to all teachers at their respective level, working toward becoming a better teacher through continuous improvement." [8]

More recently, NYSAIS has begun offering its Emerging Leaders Institute (ELI) and the Justice, Equity, and Diversity Institute (JEDI)—both of which are key events for our times.

Beginning Teacher Institute (BTI)

Starting in 1984, the BTI now serves 60 to 70 new teachers each year in two separate sessions. The BTI is designed for first- or second-year teachers and assistant teachers. The program supports professional development in three main areas:

- the self (goals, personal growth);
- the relationship to the school (parents, colleagues, heads, and students); and
- the vocation of teaching (curriculum, classroom management).

The experience is highlighted by small-group discussions led by Barbara Swanson and a seventeen-member volunteer staff, and by the videotaping of sample lessons. Participants are encouraged to identify their triumphs and misgivings in an atmosphere of good humor. The areas of focus for the BTI include:

- parent conferences;
- classroom management;
- writing comments and grades;
- setting goals;
- important issues in school today;
- working with students with learning differences
- subject-area discussions; and
- grade-level discussions. [9]

Experienced Teacher Institute (ETI)

The ETI was launched in 1994 and until five years ago it served an average of 40 teachers each year. Today, ETI has become so popular it limits enrollment to 50. Under Swanson's leadership, and staffed with three volunteer administrators and teachers from member schools, ETI participants spend three days:

- reinvigorating their teaching practice;
- reconnecting with *why* they teach;
- joining a cohort of experienced teachers;
- giving purposeful time to working on what's next;
- learning to lead as an experienced member of the community; and
- being together with other experienced teachers to learn from each other while being coached on current trends and best practices in education.

The schedule provides an opportunity for experienced teachers to:

- spend time with colleagues reflecting on their schools, their teaching, and their career paths;
- enjoy a few days in wonderful surroundings with fabulous food;
- engage in individual thought and reflection;
- examine current trends, topics, technology, and big ideas;
- meet with others in subject/grade level groups to discuss curricular issues and teaching strategies; and
- return to school with a design for a project, new approaches to familiar challenges, and a renewed outlook. [10]

Emerging Leaders Institute (ELI)

Over the past two decades, independent schools have been anticipating the importance of leadership succession planning. The planning applies not only for the head of school position and trustee leadership transitions but also to school administration, division heads, and classroom teachers.

Arising from a 2010 Think Tank—a summer residential gathering of NYSAIS staff and members from various committees—the Emerging Leaders Institute (ELI) is a confluence of a number of needs for individual teachers to support their professional growth and development, to learn about schools as institutions, and to broaden their understanding of school leadership. In doing so, the institute aims to help schools develop leaders among their staff.

For NYSAIS, the ELI emerged as a way to expand services outside of the New York City area and to push the conversation on expanding leadership opportunities for women and people of color. Finding and supporting more educational leaders is also becoming a priority with the anticipated surge of Baby Boomer heads retiring. As of this writing, the surge has already begun and will continue over the next decade.

NYSAIS describes the institute's mission this way:

> The NYSAIS Emerging Leaders Institute is designed to meet the needs of promising independent school leaders, especially women and people of color, within our member schools. This two-year cohort program engages participants with a rich curriculum that is both theoretical and practical to help them better understand schools as systems and themselves as leaders.

I was fortunate to be involved in the beginning stages of the ELI development, mostly helping in the admission process and doing some teaching. George Swain and Marcy Mann, Associate Head for Academic Affairs at The Professional Children's School in Manhattan, assembled the program and built it to where it is today. The first two-year cohort of 16 administrators and teachers began in 2011. After that cohort's resounding success, subsequent cohorts—of 18 to 20 members—have established the program as a model. A version of the ELI has been adopted by the American Montessori Society and the Pacific Northwest Association of Independent Schools.

In the spring of 2014, Swain and Mann wrote an insightful article for *Independent School*. "Learning to Lead: Lessons from the NYSAIS Emerging Leaders Institute," which drew attention to the need for supporting the growth of our newest educational leaders. [11]

Summarizing ELI's accomplishments to date, Swain says, "All graduates of the program have gone on to deepen their leadership and engagement in their schools and beyond. Of the graduates, 13 have become division heads or assistant heads of school and two have become heads of school. I hear again and again that graduates have been able to extend the independent leadership projects they began in the program into larger change initiatives in their schools."

The program has intentionally sought statewide participation. As a result, cohort members have hailed from all of the regions that NYSAIS serves, including New York City, the Hudson Valley, Westchester, Long Island, Buffalo, Rochester, and the Capital District. It has had participants from single-gender, coeducational, boarding, day, and special-needs schools. Cohort members have brought specialization in early childhood, elementary, middle school, and high school education. Participants have largely been classroom teachers and academic leaders, but they have also included admissions directors, technology directors, diversity practitioners, and communications specialists. [12]

In September 2016, the NAIS Bulletin noted an astonish-

Why Leadership Development Is Imperative for Succession Planning

September 20, 2016

AUTHOR

Donna Orem
Donna Orem is NAIS President.

"Who will lead" is a refrain we hear routinely in the media as the workforce changes hands from the Baby Boomers to the Millennials. The leading edge of the Baby Boomer generation reached retirement age in 2011. According to the Pew Research Center, 10,000 Boomers will retire each day through the year 2030. Heads of school who responded to NAIS's 2012-2013 Governance Study identified themselves primarily as Baby Boomers — 72 percent were between the ages of 50 and 69. Looking at these statistics leads me to wonder how prepared schools are for leadership transitions from one generation to the next.

ing statistic: that 10,000 Baby Boomers will retire every day through the year 2030. Of course, this means a great deal of transition for America as a whole. But it also emphasizes the need for schools to have qualified, experienced leaders ready to assume the positions that will be vacated by retiring educators. [13]

NAIS anticipated the need for leadership transition planning when it implemented its Aspiring Heads Program, which eventually became the NAIS Fellowship for Aspiring School Heads. Having been a part of the team that built the initial program back in 2003, I can fully appreciate the value of what it has done to establish the need for training our newest independent school leaders. As noted on the NAIS website, "Since 2004, the NAIS Fellowship for Aspiring School Heads has helped more than 580 women and men define and embark on their path to leadership. More than one-third of the NAIS fellows have already secured their first headship." [14]

NAIS also has its own version of NYSAIS's ELI: the NAIS School Leadership Institute. And like the ELI, it aims to help educators "cultivate an individualized professional development strategy based on your strengths and areas for improvement." [15]

I mention NAIS here to underscore the way the national, regional, and state associations of independent schools are focused on the importance of smooth, effective leadership transitions. Through BTI, ETI, ELI, and the ongoing seminars, workshops, and conferences, NYSAIS is devoted not only to supporting current heads of school but also to helping find and support the community's new and future leaders.

Justice, Equity, and Diversity Institute (JEDI)

This newest NYSAIS institute focuses on a 16-member cohort engaged in a yearlong program that equips participants to advance the work of justice, equity, and diversity in schools. The institute is led by Erica Corbin, director of community life and diversity at The Chapin School, and Yuval Ortiz-Quiroga, diversity director at Saint Anne's School, and fills a growing need to help schools become well-functioning, inclusive communities.

Workshops and Affinity Dinners

Workshops—be they one day or a series of days—are the workhorse of NYSAIS's commitment to professional development. Not only are educators personally and professional enriched by the workshops, but schools that host these workshops also present New York independent schools as a connected community devoted to providing the best education for students *and* faculty.

When I spoke with Barbara Swanson about the importance of the NYSAIS workshops—more than fifty per year—she reflected on the time in the late 1980s when she and I were planning to host the first gathering of assistant heads of school. We were debating whether to bring in a new and promising speaker based in Boston—a psychologist named Dr. Michael Thompson. Of course, Thompson turned out to be a great choice. And he would go on to speak at hundreds of schools, write numerous influential articles and best-selling books on child development and education, and become a sought-after speaker at major conferences. In 2017, for his seventieth birthday, Thompson (who, because of his engaging personality, just about everyone refers to as Michael) was honored for his lifetime achievement and his incredible impact on the independent school world. Little did we know back in the late 1980s that he'd become such an independent school icon.

Based on the many workshop offerings each month, there is no doubt that being a member of NYSAIS is most advantageous to its schools and their faculty and trustees. Every year, the demand for workshops runs high. During the month of January 2017, for example, five out of seven workshops offered were sold out. Here is a list of the workshops that were sold out:

- Crisis 101—eSeminar with Jane Hulbert
- The Power of Questions: A DBQ Approach
to Writing about History and Literature
- Diversity Education and Justice in the Curriculum
- Classroom Management For (Relatively) New
Teachers—Winter/Spring Series
- World-Mindedness Across the Curriculum

Swanson makes it clear that so much of what happens to make the conferences and institutes successful is the volunteer support that pervades the planning and hosting of each event. Not including the workshops and regional meetings that are hosted by many member schools, she estimates that, in any given year, she receives volunteer workshop support from more than 150 teachers and administrators. The NYSAIS staff could not do its job without this ongoing, generous support—not to mention the volunteer contributions from members of the NYSAIS Commission on Accreditation, the NYSAIS Board of Trustees, and other subcommittees.

What is also important to note is that NYSAIS is always looking to create new workshops, as the need arises. On its website, it even offers a form so that members can formally suggest new workshops. To ensure the workshops' success, NYSAIS also posts best practices for workshops for all the presenters.

Professional Development 2.0

As described by George Swain, "Professional Development 2.0 is extending professional development into the hybrid sphere

NYSAIS

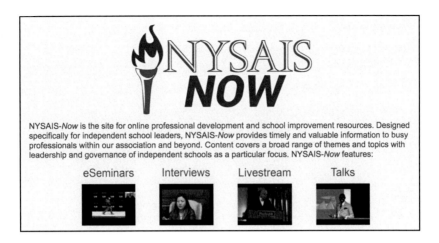

NYSAIS-*Now* is the site for online professional development and school improvement resources. Designed specifically for independent school leaders, NYSAIS-*Now* provides timely and valuable information to busy professionals within our association and beyond. Content covers a broad range of themes and topics with leadership and governance of independent schools as a particular focus. NYSAIS-*Now* features:

eSeminars   Interviews   Livestream   Talks

where educators can engage in synchronous learning (group learning happening in real time), and asynchronous learning (people learning on their own). NYSAIS *NOW* is attempting to accommodate both learning modes." [16]

In the previous chapter, I note some of the stellar features of NYAIS *NOW*. Here I want to highlight its central categories.

The NYSAIS *NOW* sections are as follows:

eSeminars

"Engage with important topics from the comfort of your own office. eSeminars are only $25, but space is limited. Please check your calendar and register for the following eSeminars today. Heads of school and trustees will find these topics to be of particular interest." [17]

Interviews

"Watch succinct, personal interviews with important educational leaders that provide prompts for discussions, meetings or individual reflection. These interviews are typically conducted with select speakers from our many wonderful conferences. Interviews will be added throughout the school year." [18]

Livestreams

"Experience selected talks by keynote conference speakers in real-time throughout the year. Attend one (or all) of our outstanding NYSAIS residential conferences without leaving the comfort of your home or office. No registration is required. Simply set aside the time and go to the NYSAIS *NOW* Livestream page at *new.livestream.com/nysaislive* to participate." [19]

Talks

"Find outstanding conference talks archived on the NYSAIS *NOW* website for your use when you need them. Watch past Livestream conference speakers when you have the time available. Share with others in a faculty or trustee meeting. Send a link to a colleague." [20]

It's hard to overstate the value of NYSAIS *NOW*—not only how it serves member schools today but also how it will evolve to serve members in the future. At the same time, NYSAIS is clearly dedicated to in-person events. For now, this blended-learning environment is ideal for meeting the varied and important needs of the members.

As the technology evolves, it's clear the site will grow by leaps and bounds.

CHAPTER SIX

Independence, Inspiration, and Innovation Beyond 70 Years

The title for this book—*Design for Independence, Inspiration, and Innovation: NYSAIS at 70*—reflects what I think of as the heart of NYSAIS today. To start, it reflects the organizational mindset for design. "Design," as Steve Jobs once said, "is not just what it looks like and feels like. Design is how it *works*." [1]

NYSAIS is an organization designed and constantly recalibrated by the staff for its own independence, inspiration, and innovation, as well as that of its member schools.

When I think about independence, I think of organizational guru Stephen Covey, who once said, "Every human has four endowments—self awareness, conscience, independent will, and creative imagination. These give us the ultimate human freedom . . . The power to choose, to respond, to change." [2] These are all qualities that independent schools want for their graduates. They are also coveted institutional qualities. In a 21st-century context, organizational independence is as much about creative imagination as it is about self-governance. NYSAIS is an excellent example of a high-functioning independent organization. Of course, it is also focused on defending, supporting, and guiding the essential independence of its members.

NYSAIS also understands inspiration. By being connected to so many experts and thought leaders in education, the staff itself is inspired to develop an ever-evolving professional development program, which in turn inspires schools to be their best. Inspiration isn't just about ideas. It is about generating ideas in the context of deep knowledge of the past, fact-based understanding of the needs of the present, and a clear future direction based on mission. "I have great respect for the past," wrote poet Maya Angelou. "If you don't know where you've come from, you don't know where you're going. I have respect for the past, but I'm a person of the moment. I'm here, and I do my best to be completely centered at the place I'm at, then I go forward to the next place." [3]

There are lessons in Angelou's perspective for all of us in education: know your history, know your mission, but also be as present as you can in the moment.

Of course, smart innovation is required today if schools want to stay relevant in the years and decades to come. There are hundreds of books on innovation. There are institutes and conferences dedicated to the topic. But I find myself thinking mostly about innovation as creative adaptability. Alexandra Adornetto, an Australian children's book author, once wrote, "Imagination and invention go hand in hand. Remember how lack of resources was never a problem in childhood games? Shift a few pieces of furniture around the living room, and you have yourself a fort." [4]

Schools have to be inventive today—especially with the pressures to adapt to technological and cultural changes, but also in their approach to the business of being a school, to keeping costs down and thinking wisely about mission-based allocation of funds, and in guiding their evolving curricula. Writing in *Independent School*, Judy Sheridan highlighted a central challenge for independent schools and the associations that support them:

> The question, "What is a school?" has become commonplace today, as has the language of "disruptive innovation." Brick-and-mortar classrooms and libraries are increasingly viewed as old school. Instead, there are new schools without walls, online and blended-learning programs offering synchronous and asynchronous teaching, and information and media centers that give students more agency in their own learning. With tablets in hand, many students independently complete their academic work, no longer depending on a teacher in front of the classroom or even beside them in a learning circle. [5]

The fact that NYSAIS is well aware of these disruptive changes in education speaks volumes for the organization. This awareness has enabled NYSAIS to evolve well with the times. Its ability to adapt to the swirl of disruption and revolutionary changes in the culture and education in the past three years, in particular, suggests that its future will be strong. There is no better book that addresses how disruption fosters innovation than Clayton Christensen's *The Innovator's Dilemma*. [6]

In fact, the recent NYSAIS initiatives are a guiding star for the organization's future. Continuing to defend the independence of its members, inspire schools to evolve and grow in order to remain excellent and relevant institutions, and to showcase and push for innovation in education is NYSAIS's direction and passion.

As highlighted earlier, NYSAIS is well aware of its need to embrace technology with all that it has to offer. The staff also understands the power and importance of another 21st-century skill: collaboration. Whether it involves connection with one of the thirty-plus state and regional independent school associations, the National Association of Independent Schools (NAIS), the Council for American Private Education (CAPE), the American Montessori Society (AMS), or some other education organization, NYSAIS is committed to looking beyond its state borders to bring the best educational services to its members.

In March 2017, to take one example, Mark Lauria, Barbara Swanson, Judy Sheridan, and George Swain traveled to China to speak at a symposium for the Online Education Strategies for Independent Schools (OESIS) group. OESIS is a dynamic network of more than 550 independent schools and more than 2,500 leading innovators in education. The group "focuses on changing the learning models of schools with an emphasis on the innovative practices in pedagogy, curriculum development, and school culture change." [7] The NYSAIS team was invited to the Beijing symposium to share its insights, expertise, and practices related to the accreditation process. At the same time, the staff would connect with this engaging group of globally minded educators. What they learn on these outings always finds a way into the services NYSAIS offers.

Among those key services today are the professional development opportunities, particularly in the areas of leadership cultivation, good governance, and school finance. These are not independent topics to be addressed separately. NYSAIS understands that they are inextricably linked. As Sheridan also notes in her *Independent School* article, "Recognizing that the

George, Judy, Barbara, and Mark with China delegation

future of a school relies on the application of the most rigorous standards in governance and finance, the process moves to self-reflection that addresses the viability of the institution by examining the practices in these areas." [8]

Ultimately, I believe that the best way to assess NYSAIS's future is to go right to the heart of the matter—the staff. In a discussion with the staff, I asked the question in the midst of NYSAIS's seventieth birthday, "One of the last things I want to talk about is the future. Where are we going from here? Where will NYSAIS be at seventy-five? Where will it be at eighty?"

Among the issues the staff raised is the question of staff diversity. "I think our staff will need to be more diverse than it is as we go forward," Swanson said. This understanding is related directly to the growing diversity of students and faculty in schools as well as to the evolving diversity of the broader culture and the need for a multicultural curriculum. Independent schools have a history of being predominately white. But that is changing—for cultural reasons, educational reasons, and social justice reasons. NYSAIS and other education associations need to diversify their staff in order to serve increasingly diverse schools well.

Another hope is that NYSAIS continues to explore its approach to organizational evolution so that it remains, as Sheridan put it, "entwined with the very future of independent school education." One way to do this is for NYSAIS to continue to provide a strong mix of professional development workshops and conferences, offer support services to school leaders, and maintain an accreditation process that continues to bolster independent schools. It also means that NYSAIS will continue to rely on the volunteer services of many members.

In terms of technology, the NYSAIS staff knows it will need to continue to create new applications and programs enabled by technology. But it will also need to support personal connections and professional relationships within the community. With the help of technology, the staff also wants to continue to break down boundaries between schools as well as between schools and the broader educational world. For its part, NYSAIS continues to improve relationships with other independent school associations for cross-pollination of ideas.

On the latter topic, Swain said, "We have developed strong connections with people in other associations, and we collaborate with them. We are also learning from them." A perfect example is the way NYSAIS is learning about how other school associations engage in data analytics and strategic work based on this data.

Mark Lauria summed up the staff's approach to evolving the organization's services now and in the years to come. "As strategic thinkers, we are always looking at what's out there. We're scanning the environment. I don't think any of us are afraid to take a risk and give it a try. If something works, that's great. If it doesn't, well we move on."

How fortunate that NYSAIS's leadership throughout the past seventy years has lead it schools to such a strong position of independence, inspiration, and innovation through strong leadership from a dedicated staff and devoted volunteers. This leadership will undoubtedly prevail over the next seventy years.

ACKNOWLEDGMENTS

What a great joy it has been to research and write *Design for Independence, Inspiration, and Innovation: The New York State Association of Independent Schools at 70*. As I think about the many books I have had the pleasure to read, the two that capture the essence of *this* book are Jim Collins's *Good to Great* and *Good to Great and the Social Sectors*. NYSAIS could easily have been the poster child for the latter book. Over the past seventy years, NYSAIS has evolved from a good association into a truly great one. Particularly impressive is the way NYSAIS has evolved in the first decade and a half of the 21st century — the time period covered here. In order to make this happen, it has taken a strong, dedicated team and determined, thoughtful leaders.

Thanks and recognition go to Mark W. Lauria, executive director of NYSAIS, who has lead the way admirably. Thanks and recognition also go to the NYSAIS staff — Andrew S. Cooke, Maria Flores Seibert, Judy Sheridan, George Swain, Barbara Swanson, and Diana Wahrlich — who have provided the accuracy and foundation of the content. Having a strong team to draw upon in writing the book made the task meaningful, rewarding, and satisfying.

The mechanics of putting the book together could not have been done without my writing partner and editor, Michael Brosnan. He has been my writing guide and teacher throughout the process and over the past twenty-five years. Susan Gold helped bring about the visual design of the book so that readers can connect the text with form. I appreciate their expertise and hard work.

Finally, I offer much love and thanks to Chris and our beautiful family who accommodated and supported the innumerable hours of work it took to make *Design for Independence, Inspiration, and Innovation* a reality.

NOTES

INTRODUCTION

1 Orem, Donna, "Why Leadership Development Is Imperative for Succession Planning," The *Independent School* Magazine Blog, September 21, 2016.

2 NYSAIS website: *www.nysais.org/page.cfm?p=2862*.

3 Peters, Dane L., *Independent by Design*, 2014, pp. 59-60.

4 NYSAIS website: *www.nysais.org/page.cfm?p=2880*.

CHAPTER ONE Finding the Virtual and Personal Balance

1 Pink, Daniel, *Drive: The Surprising Truth About What Motivates Us*, Riverhead Books, New York, 2009, pp. 86-87.

2 Zoom Video Conferencing and Web Conferencing Service website: *www.zoom.us/*.

3 NYSAIS Staff meeting transcript, March 15, 2017, p. 4.

4 NYSAIS Staff meeting transcript, March 15, 2017, p. 9.

5 Steiner-Adair, Catherine, *The Big Disconnect*, Harper Collins, New York, 2013, p. 18.

6 Lauria, Mark W., Ph.D., "Using Technology to Increase Communication," *The Trustee's Letter*, September/October 2015.

7 NYSAIS Staff meeting transcript, March 15, 2017, pp. 8-9.

CHAPTER TWO Evolving Member Services

1 *What's Happening Now @ NYSAIS Newsletter*, April 2017: *http://us14.campaign-archive2.com/?u=7a6633593e3d6e ea6793e8569&id=1438e43932&e=f8c8909f61*.

2 Lauria, Mark, interview with Dane Peters, May 6, 2017.

3 NYSAIS website "Hybrid Learning": *www.nysais.org/page.cfm?p=3095.*

4 NYSAIS website "ELAS": *www.nysais.org/page.cfm?p=3195.*

5 NYSAIS website "Best Practices": *www.nysais.org/page.cfm?p=3096.*

6 Lauria, Mark, interview with Dane Peters, June 2, 2017.

7 Peters, Dane L., *Independent by Design*, 2014, pp. 59-60.

CHAPTER THREE Strengthening Schools Through Accreditation

1 Lauria, Mark W., Ph.D., "What Is Accreditation?," *The Parents League of New York Review 2016.*

2 Sheridan, Judith, "Transformation Through Accreditation," *Independent School*, Spring 2016, p. 51.

3 NAIS website "Commission on Accreditation": *www.nais.org/About/Pages/Commission-on-Accreditation.aspx?src=footer.*

4 Sheridan, Judith, "Transformation Through Accreditation," *Independent School*, Spring 2016, p. 52.

CHAPTER FOUR Technology and the Future of Schools

1 Peters, Dane L., *Independent by Design*, 2014, p. 103.

2 NYSAIS Staff meeting transcript, March 15, 2017, p. 6.

3 Cooke, Andrew, Email to Dane Peters, May 4, 2017.

4 NYSAIS Staff meeting transcript, March 15, 2017, p. 5.

5 NAIS website DASL: *http://dasl.nais.org/?src=submenu.*

6 NYSAIS website: *www.nysais.org.*

7 NYSAIS Staff meeting transcript, March 15, 2017, pp. 14-15.

8 Ibid. p. 13.

9 Lauria, Mark W., Ph.D., "Using Technology to Increase Communication," *The Trustee's Letter*, September/October 2015.

CHAPTER FIVE Professional Development

1   NBC Nightly News with Lester Holt, April 27, 2016.

2   "The Grandparent Boom," *AARP Bulletin*, May 2017, p. 4.

3   The Center for Generational Kinetics website: *http:// genhq.com/faq-info-about-generations/*.

4   *Professional Development Exchange*, Fall 1989.

5   NYSAIS website: *www.nysais.org/page.cfm?p=3184*.

6   Lane, Chester, "Listen, Learn, and Lead," *Symphony*, January-February 2010, pp. 26-28.

7   Nierenberg, Roger, *Maestro: A Surprising Story About Leading By Listening*, Portfolio, 2009.

8   NYSAIS website: *www.nysais.org/page.cfm?p=3661*.

9   NYSAIS website: *www.nysais.org/page.cfm?id=3094&start=10/06/2016&verbose=13344*.

10 NYSAIS website: *www.nysais.org/page.cfm?id=3094&start=05/06/2018&verbose=13472*.

11 Mann, Marcy and Swain, George, "Learning to Lead: Lessons from the NYSAIS Emerging Leaders Institute," *Independent School*, Spring 2014.
    NAIS website: *www.nais.org/Magazines-Newsletters/IS Magazine/Pages/Learning-to-Lead.aspx*.

12 Swain, George, interview with Dane Peters, May 15, 2017.

13 *NAIS Bulletin*, Independent Ideas Blog, "The Succession Planning Imperative," September 21, 2016.

14 NAIS website: *www.nais.org/participate/fellowship-for-aspiring-school-heads/*.

15 NAIS website: *www.nais.org/participate/institutes-work shops/school-leadership-institute/?_cldee=ZGFuZUBue XNhaXMub3Jn&recipientid=contact-41f10c5649cf 4c4890d51c132d55f5e4-a6874605b7e24a74a4c485abea08 978f&esid=da7f133d-6224-e711-a031-005056bf0011*.

16 Swain, George, interview with Dane Peters, April 21, 2017.

17 NYSAIS website: *www.nysais.org/page.cfm?p=3509#esem inars/?p=3509.*

18 NYSAIS website: *www.nysais.org/page.cfm?p=3352#inter views/?p=3352.*

19 NYSAIS website: *www.nysais.org/page.cfm?p=3510.*

20 NYSAIS website: *www.nysais.org/page.cfm?p=3622#talks /?p=3622.*

CHAPTER SIX Independence, Inspiration, and Innovation Beyond 70 Years

1 BrainyQuote website: *www.brainyquote.com/quotes/ quotes/s/stevejobs169129.html.*

2 BrainyQuote website: *www.brainyquote.com/quotes/ quotes/s/stephencov138246.html?src=t_independence.*

3 BrainyQuote website: *www.brainyquote.com/quotes/ quotes/m/mayaangelo634505.html.*

4 BrainyQuote website: *www.brainyquote.com/quotes/ quotes/a/alexandraa725168.html?src=t_imagination.*

5 Sheridan, Judith, "Transformation Through Accreditation," *Independent School*, Spring 2016, p. 50.

6 Christensen, Clayton, *Innovator's Dilemma*, Harper Business Essentials, New York, NY, 2003.

7 Online Education Strategies for Independent Schools (OESIS) website: *www.oesisgroup.com/?page_id=428& tab=5.*

8 Sheridan, Judith, "Transformation Through Accreditation," *Independent School*, Spring 2016, p. 51.